I WANT TO BE A
JOURNALIST

Written by
Valerie Poh

Edited by
Jonathan Reule

Illustration
Carlos Varejão

Storyboard
Keziah Gan

First paperback edition October 2023
ISBN 978-981-17359-6-7

Published by Unibino Pte. Ltd.
9 North Buona Vista Drive, #02-01 Metropolis Tower 1, Singapore 138588

www.unibino.com

Journalists are the great messengers of our modern world. These professionals not only find unique and interesting stories to bring to us but also serve as the guardians of truth and accountability. Their dedication to seeking the truth and presenting unbiased information is essential for a well-informed society.
LA NAZIONE
ABC-1234

Are you passionate about empowering others with knowledge and providing accurate information? Do you have a keen interest in uncovering compelling stories and serving as a trusted source of information for the public? If you answered 'Yes!' to both, then a career in journalism may be the perfect fit for you.

But before we get ahead of ourselves, why don't we first take a look into our past to better understand how this career formed? If we go all the way back to prehistoric times, when humans first walked the Earth, we'll find a very different way of life than what we have today.

We had no TVs, radios, or computers to give us instant access to information. Instead, we had to rely on other humans and animals for information about current events. But why was it so important for us to know what was happening in our world? Why did we need to be up to date with news reports, even back in prehistoric times?

Let's imagine for a minute; you're living in prehistoric times, and you're out hunting when you see a pride of lions near your village, looking for their next meal. Now, what would you do in this situation? Would you keep the information to yourself, or would you rush back to alert your village of the impending danger?

Like many others, you would likely hurry back to your village to inform your family and friends about the presence of lions nearby. By doing so, you would be providing your community with important and timely news that they can use to stay safe and make necessary preparations for the lions roaming in their vicinity.

As you might be starting to see from this example, having current and up-to-date news reports was often a key to our survival in the long ago past. But these reports weren't only related to dangerous events, they also included news of better plots of land that villagers could migrate to.

It could also be a message about upcoming weather based on observations. Or even where a new supply of food was located. No matter the content, news reports have been occurring for almost as long as we've been on this Earth!

Over time, these bearers of news came to be known as messengers. In fact, the role of a messenger became an official position in various ancient civilizations. Their responsibilities included giving information to the public about newly enacted laws by the government, as well as providing updates on wars and battles taking place.

Messengers also played a crucial role in informing people about various aspects of daily life. They would relay news about trade and commerce activities, keeping the community updated on new trade agreements, changes in taxes, and even the arrival of foreign goods in town. It was like having an insider's preview of what was new and exciting in the market! Their valuable insights helped people stay connected and make informed decisions in their daily lives.

However, there were also differences in how ancient civilisations spread the news. In ancient China, for example, news was shared through written notices and public announcements. These important messages were prominently displayed in places where people gathered, such as bustling markets, revered temples, and prominent government buildings.

In addition to their methods of spreading news through written notices and public announcements, the ancient Chinese had a highly organized system of messengers. These messengers played a crucial role in delivering messages and announcements from the emperor to people across vast distances. Whether on horseback or by boat, the messengers were carefully chosen for their exceptional speed, endurance, and unwavering loyalty. Extensive training prepared them for the arduous journeys required to ensure the timely delivery of important information to communities far and wide.

Continuing our journey through ancient civilizations, we arrive in Ancient Rome, where the concept of regular publication took shape. Enter the "acta diurna," daily gazettes that revolutionized the spread of information. These handwritten publications, crafted on parchment or papyrus, were prominently displayed in public spaces. Acting as a valuable source of knowledge, the acta diurna offered updates on various subjects, including government affairs, military exploits, and the latest news of the day.

Furthermore, in the vibrant streets of ancient Rome, public speaking took centre stage as a powerful medium for delivering news and information.

Esteemed politicians and influential figures would captivate the masses with their oratory skills, utilizing grand public spaces like the Forum Romanum. Just picture the scene—a multitude of people assembling in large crowds, eagerly awaiting the latest updates and announcements. It resembled an ancient rendition of a modern-day press conference or news briefing, where important news was shared, opinions were voiced, and the collective pulse of the city was felt.

Continuing into the Middle Ages, journalism underwent two significant advancements: the rise of news pamphlets and the invention of the printing press. News pamphlets, resembling small booklets, emerged as a new form of disseminating current events. Although written by anonymous individuals and not always the most trustworthy source of information, they offered a more accessible and expedient means of news delivery compared to traditional methods like oral communication or handwritten documents.

However, the real game-changer was the printing press, a revolutionary invention that allowed for the mass production of written materials, without requiring each copy of the material to be handwritten! With the printing press, news dissemination became faster and more widespread, which laid the foundation for modern journalism as we know it today.

In the wake of the printing press's revolutionary impact, a new era of journalism emerged, forever transforming the way information was shared and consumed. Newspapers, brimming with articles, stories, and opinions, started to grace the hands of eager readers.

With the ability to produce multiple copies quickly and efficiently, journalists could now report on a wide range of topics, from local news to global events. Readers eagerly awaited the latest editions, hungry for knowledge and insight. The printing press paved the way for the vibrant world of modern journalism, where information flows freely, empowering individuals with the power of knowledge.

James Augustus Hicky, a pioneering figure in the history of journalism, is widely hailed as the father of modern journalism. In the late 18th century, Hicky established the first-ever newspaper in India called 'Hicky's Bengal Gazette' or 'The Original Calcutta General Advertiser.' This revolutionary publication marked a significant turning point in the world of journalism.

Hicky's newspaper was bold, innovative, and unafraid to challenge the status quo. He fearlessly exposed corruption, highlighted social issues, and championed the principles of free press and freedom of expression. Hicky's Bengal Gazette paved the way for a new era of journalism that prioritized investigative reporting, critical analysis, and holding those in power accountable.

Now that you have delved into the captivating stories of influential journalists throughout history, it's natural to wonder how you can embark on your own path as a modern-day storyteller and an agent of change. Luckily, there are various avenues to pursue a career in journalism today.

One of the most common routes is to pursue a journalism degree. Numerous universities and colleges offer undergraduate and graduate programs specifically tailored to equip aspiring journalists with the necessary skills and knowledge. These comprehensive programs delve into various facets of journalism, including reporting, writing, editing, and multimedia production.

In addition to formal education, embracing opportunities for hands-on experience can greatly enrich your journey towards becoming a journalist. Seeking internships or freelance assignments with newspapers, magazines, online publications, or broadcast outlets allows you to hone your skills, build a portfolio, and establish valuable connections within the industry.

As you continue to delve into the captivating world of journalism and contemplate your future in this dynamic field, it's crucial to recognize the vast array of avenues available for exploration.

Within the realm of journalism, you'll discover an assortment of paths that might align with your unique interests and skill sets, allowing you to embark on a fulfilling career tailored to your passions.

One such avenue is the captivating realm of print journalism, where words come alive on paper or screen as you weave compelling narratives that captivate readers. Through the written word, print journalists have the power to inform, entertain, and enlighten, shaping the stories that grace the pages of newspapers, magazines, and other printed materials.

Whether it's delving into the latest developments in entertainment, dissecting the intricacies of sports, dissecting political landscapes, or unearthing compelling local stories, print journalists serve as the conduits, bringing timely and engaging news to their readers.

As a broadcast journalist, you step into the heart of the action, immersing yourself in the stories that shape our world. Your role encompasses various captivating responsibilities, from reporting on breaking news from the field to anchoring news broadcasts and delivering crucial headlines to viewers and listeners alike. With every on-screen appearance, your words and presence carry the weight of informing, enlightening, and engaging audiences in real time.

If you have a burning passion for justice and a natural inclination for unearthing hidden truths, investigative journalism beckons as a path where your sleuthing skills can make a profound impact on the world. At its core, investigative journalism is the art of unravelling the concealed layers behind a specific topic or issue.

As an investigative journalist, you embark on a relentless pursuit of truth, dedicating countless hours to meticulously examine documents, interview sources, and follow leads that hold the potential to unveil the untold story.

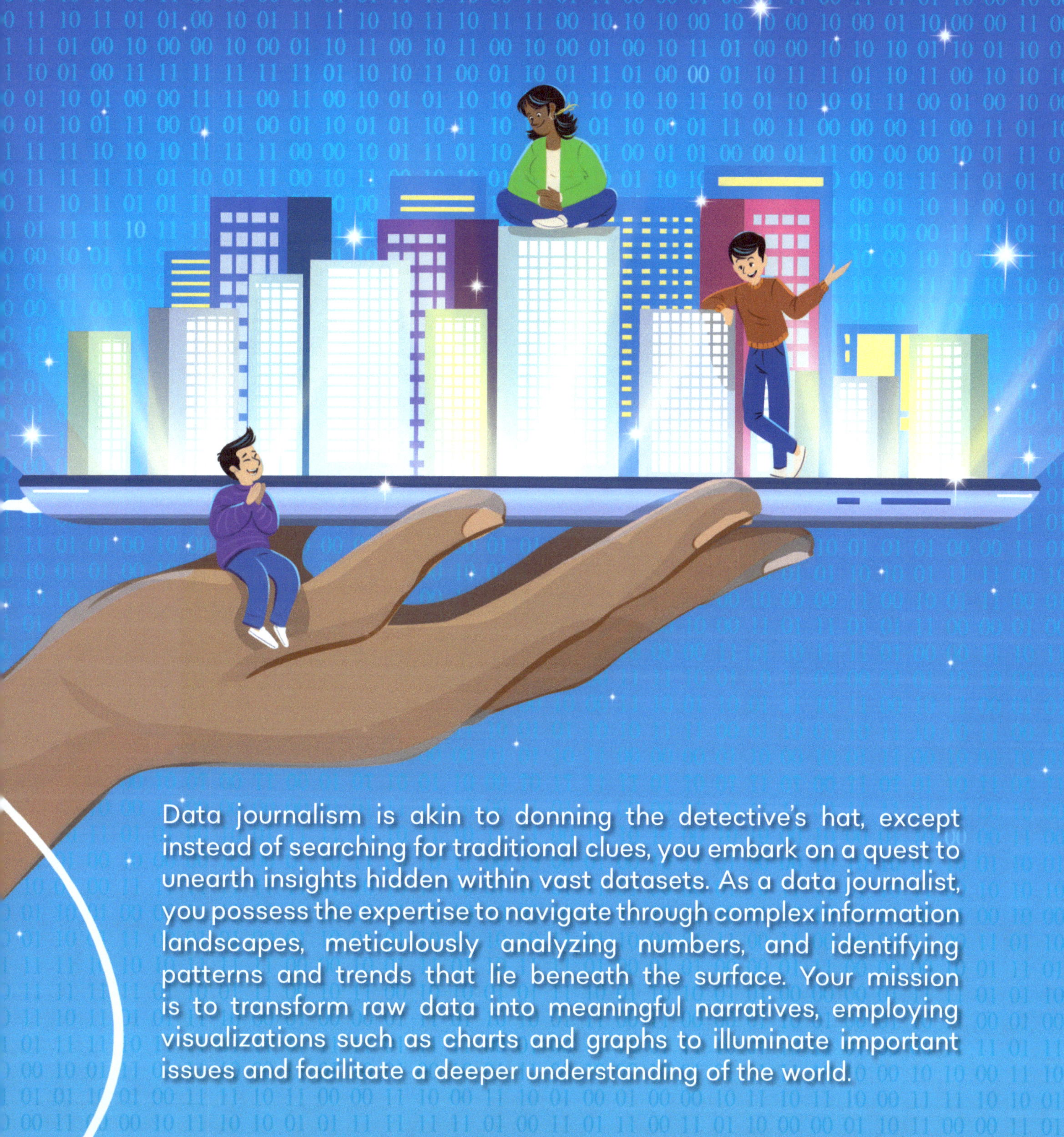

Data journalism is akin to donning the detective's hat, except instead of searching for traditional clues, you embark on a quest to unearth insights hidden within vast datasets. As a data journalist, you possess the expertise to navigate through complex information landscapes, meticulously analyzing numbers, and identifying patterns and trends that lie beneath the surface. Your mission is to transform raw data into meaningful narratives, employing visualizations such as charts and graphs to illuminate important issues and facilitate a deeper understanding of the world.

In the diverse landscape of journalism, myriad paths await those passionate about uncovering truth and sharing it with the world. As you embark on your journey as a journalist, know that you hold the power to make a significant impact through your work. Whether you choose the path of print journalism, broadcast journalism, investigative journalism, data journalism, or any other avenue within this vibrant field, your ultimate mission remains unchanged.

So, as you embark on this exhilarating journey, remember that journalism is not merely a career but a calling. Embrace the opportunities to explore different avenues, sharpen your skills, and uncover stories that deserve to be told. Let your passion for truth, justice, and the power of words guide you as you strive to make a difference, one article, one report, and one conversation at a time.

My Inspiration

Shubhi Saxena
Founder, Unibino

As a parent in this ever-changing world, it can sometimes feel overwhelming when it comes to our children's futures. New technologies seem to be arising almost every day, and with so many innovations, it creates unique professions which many of us wouldn't have dreamed to be necessary only a few years ago. Which to me is a good thing. Because with so much variety, my children can have the opportunity to pick a career that will fit their personalities and build upon their strengths. As you may imagine, this desire within me to provide my children with the resources they needed to thrive, led me to search out books that would be easy enough for them to understand while teaching them about various professions.

Only, I found that these books were few and far between. Even if I could find a book about a certain profession geared towards young readers, I found them sparse inside and limited to only certain careers that may not fit my children's abilities. This is when I came up with the idea to write my own children's books, teaching them about all the various careers in the modern world. After months of researching different professions and learning more than I ever expected, I quickly realised this was going to be a bigger project than I first anticipated. I dove into the histories of these professions, discovering links to the past, and why these professions were now so important.

Ultimately my goal was to offer my children options, to show them that there is no one set path for everyone. But in this, I stumbled upon something bigger. I wanted to share this with future generations. To share with all children and parents about these careers, to help spark curiosity, and to instil a passion for the future. Everyone has special talents and abilities, and I hope that this series will be able to offer clarity and inspiration to children around the world. Because at the end of the day, it's never too early to start dreaming and never too late to take action. With this, I hope you enjoy this series and that your young ones become the best versions of themselves as they can achieve.